RECIPE FOR LIFE

MAKING THE MOST OF THE FORKS IN THE ROAD

BY DEBBIE GORE

Lori
Celebrate
life
every day!

Happy Birthday!

— Debbie Gore
4/10/2011

To contact Debbie Gore for an interview, signed copies of books or to hire her to speak:
Debbie@recipeforlife.biz
www.recipeforlife.biz
817-329-8538
P.O. Box 952
Grapevine, Texas 76099

About the author: Debbie Gore is a speaker, chef and author whose previous career as a fashion buyer for Fortune 500 companies included Dillard's Department Stores, A Pea in the Pod and Viacom Entertainment. Her own forks in the road helped prepare her to succeed in fulfilling her dream and passion to help others develop their potential. She authored the cookbook series, *Good Friends Great Tastes*, managed culinary schools and served as the Director of Culinary Services for an international high-tech oven company.

To David, my very patient husband.
With our daily commitment and
connection, all things seem possible.
Love,
Debbie

ACKNOWLEDGEMENTS

After my father Louie passed away, I found this quote on his desk: *"The way to happiness: keep your heart free from hate, your mind free from worry. Live simply, expect little, give much. Fill your life with love. Scatter sunshine. Forget self, think of others. Do as you would be done by."* – Unknown. Thanks, Dad.

Thank you to all my friends, family and new acquaintances that I meet daily who fill my life with love.

With gratitude and heartfelt love, I thank my husband Dave and my son Ryan for their humor and support while I wrote *Recipe for Life.*

Thank you David and Linda Gore for the opportunity to work at Caviar to Cabernet. Who would have imagined it would be such a life-changing experience?

Thank you Audrey Scherer for designing a book cover that inspired my writing every step of the way! www.audreyschererphotography.com

Thank you to Melissa Weikel, Ed Bamberger, Marla Payne, Becky Loboda and Erin Bailey for your meticulous editing, insight and continuous encouragement. Each one of you helped me clarify my message and believed in my vision. Special thanks to Marla for coaching me on my speaking and to Erin for our multi-generational friendship that has taught me the joy of Twitter!

Thank you to my mother and father who helped me see the contrasts and struggles of love, sacrifice and communication. To my mother Brigitte, who introduced me to self-help books at a young age and my father, Louie, who rarely had a bad day until his struggle with Alzheimer's.

Thank you God for keeping my IGS tuned in!

Thank you to those of you that have gifted me with inspirational sayings and recipes. Thanks to all of you that have supported my aspirations and taught me many life lessons. Keep them coming!

In joy,

Debbie Gore

Email: Debbie@recipeforlife.biz
Twitter: @recipeforlife

TABLE OF CONTENTS

Meats

Pasta

Vegetables

Desserts

CHAPTER 1:
TAKE THE FIRST BITE

The very first feelings you ever felt, before you were even fully *you*, were hunger and thirst. We begin life craving nourishment, then we hunger for adventure, for connection, for success, for love. As soon as we're born we thirst for milk, and as we evolve we thirst for inner peace and greater purpose.

Every day we feed these cravings with the ingredients that fill our lives (some healthy, some indulgent, some unhealthy). Your body tells you how to quench your physical thirsts with fruit smoothies or an ice-cold beer. This book will help you develop the instincts to feed a different hunger: the cravings of your heart and soul.

We'll examine the never-ending choices that life throws our way – family, career, friends, finances, health – and together, help you create a Recipe for Life filled with ingredients that bring <u>you</u> satisfaction and joy. (Plus, we'll help you discard any harmful ingredients that you'd like to remove from your daily plate!).

As you read this book, completing the exercises and writing your Recipe for Life, I hope you'll reach out to others like you on our blog (www.recipefor-life.biz/blog) and Facebook (www.facebook.com/recipeforlife). You'll find men and women from all walks of life exploring their recipes together. Welcome to the table!

Let's Begin with a Picture

Let's begin with a picture. You: age six.

Remember? Life was full of possibilities, surprises and beckoning adventures. You could read the kids' menu and choose treats for yourself. But life was also full of rules. Every time your parents said, "No!" did you think: *someday I'll have the freedom to do EVERYTHING?*

Then, suddenly, you were 16, 26, 36... Suddenly, adults didn't seem so free and powerful anymore. I catch myself sometimes longing for the freedom of childhood, no worries, no car payments, no counting calories. Life is no longer simple; it's a vast menu of overwhelming choices. Forks in the road are much more daunting now. There are no parents to constrain your choices. It's just you and the fork.

Decision time. What should you choose? The more choices available to you, the more pressure you feel.

Picture yourself today. Is this the life you ordered off the menu? Have you ever thought, "I wish I could send it back?"

I did!

Years ago, simple key ingredients were missing from my life. I worked first as a fashion buyer for several retail chains, making million-dollar decisions, but I was not satisfied or happy. I was spending much more time thinking about what I wanted for lunch than what I wanted for my life.

How could I find happiness? Did I have a choice?

Who would guess a job layoff and a divorce would be my forks in the road. Now, what path should I take? Had I created a recipe for disaster?

But it was these ingredients for disaster that showed me the way to "Recipe for Life". First, I took a temp job at a gourmet store. The work at the store was not the crazy pace I was used to – but I loved it! Because the days were filled with two of my newly discovered passions: working with people and connecting to them through food. I also reveled in my newfound freedom and entrepreneurial spirit. A different life came into focus.

I began to look for ingredients that I could change in my life. In the evenings after work, I focused on a cookbook project. While gathering, testing and writing recipes, I reconnected with my creativity, which put me on a whole new path of consciousness. I became aware of how my choice to engage in this project made me feel a sense of joy and light-heartedness that had been missing from my life. There, I discovered that by adding a dash of passion here, a pinch of perseverance there, and seeking the right combination of ingredients, I could design my own life recipe.

"You cannot change your destination overnight, but you can change your direction."

Jim Rohn

Over the next few weeks, my heart raced as I tasted and tested my own Recipe for Life. Suddenly, fresh ideas and personal discoveries bubbled to the surface.

As I crafted my recipe, I realized:

1. Recipes are written with the most important ingredients listed first. Without the chicken, a Chicken Parmesan just isn't satisfying – no matter how tasty the cheese and tomatoes. The same goes for life! Until I satisfied the needs closest to my heart (relationship and career), I couldn't embrace the smaller joys.

2. If a recipe calls for an ingredient that's missing from your pantry, you can be creative! Some of my most delicious concoctions were cooked because I didn't have all the "right" ingredients. Instead of waiting for life to deliver the perfect spice, I started improvising. New interests. New ways to do simple everyday chores. I joined new

associations and read more books. My brain started thinking more creatively and recognizing more opportunities than I had ever seen before.

3. I choose recipes with ingredients I like. I never force myself to eat something if I don't care for the taste. Simple, right? So why did I choose so many things for my <u>life</u> that *didn't* make me happy? Life should consist of only the ingredients we like. I gave myself the freedom to discard or replace the ingredients that were spoiling the recipe. Have a group of friends who never ask you a question, but share plenty of their life happenings? Don't call them as frequently. Have you been to lunch with whining coworkers whose negativity left your feeling drained? Make alternate arrangements. Don't let unhealthy ingredients consume your life!

4. Chefs and foodies know that the tastiest meals usually come from the highest-quality ingredients. That's why we enjoy the recipes again and again. As I tasted, mixed, matched and eliminated ingredients for my life, I knew they had to be as nourishing as possible.

The challenge: choosing what you want to keep and what you're ready to discard. What makes you happiest in life? We'll spend the rest of this chapter helping you identify the best ingredients for your recipe!

Try this. Think about the things you put on your to-do list each day or week. If you find things that are jobs instead of joys is there a way to improve them? For some of us, including me, staying accountable can be a "job". Did we exercise? Did we follow up on the marketing materials or the leads we received?

I find the earlier in the day that I tackle the difficult things, the easier it is. When you get things done early in the day, that aren't your favorite, your day is assured to just get better and better.

It helps to have an accountability partner. Tell your partner what goals you have and let them do the same. Work on the same goal together. Completing difficult challenges becomes much easier when you have a partner in joy!

Exercise 1: Joy or Job?

Everything I Did Today:	When?	Add Joy to each job
Clean house	8 a.m. M	Listen to a book on tape
Power walk	6 a.m. T-T 8 a.m. S-S	Walk with partner
Make follow-up calls	9:30 a.m. T-F	This time works for me!

How many "jobs" can you convert to "joys?" The next few exercises will help you do just that. Begin with small incremental improvements that enhance your life. Tiny consistent changes in your daily routine over time will create better days, months and years.

Exercise #2: Out with the Old

What are three things that you would like to eliminate (or delegate)?

1.
2.
3.

Give yourself permission to stop doing things that drain your energy. Figure out the core reasons *why* they drain you so much. Can you delegate or remove them from your life? Can you convert them into joys?

For me there were things my professional life that needed improvement. I did not enjoy nor was I meticulous in keeping up with the finances of a business and my personal expenses. I asked a friend who is an independent office assistant if I could pay her to do so. Every few weeks, she comes by the house to pick up my inbox and she records it and files the paperwork. At tax time it is a huge relief. I was trying to improve on a weakness by overcoming it, but felt more and more frustrated trying to manage this myself. Instead, I decided to allow a professional to take over this task so I could develop my strengths instead of focusing on overcoming my weakness!

Consult Your IGS

Following your Recipe for Life ~ consistently choosing the good ingredients and avoiding the bad ones ~ will help you make decisions much more easily. You'll develop an intuitive sense of what "feels" right to you. Your decisions will start as thoughts, then travel to your heart and end up in your core, where gut feelings simmer. A bad decision may cause you to have a headache, heartburn or a stomach ache. That is your body speaking to you – and you should listen.

I call it the IGS. Internal Guidance System. Just as your Global Positioning System (GPS) navigates the highway, your own IGS helps you navigate your life. Your internal map will light up with roads to lead you to your life's missing ingredients.

"Listen to your gut feeling, it is often a very good mouthpiece for the heart."

J.M. Hurley

Check Your Awareness Meter

Check your "awareness" meter by answering this one question: Have you ever looked at your caller ID and made the decision not to take the call? Maybe you decided to call the person back later because you were not in the mood to talk or the timing was inconvenient. You stopped to think about who was calling, and your heart judged the scenario based on how it felt. Your gut feeling reassured you that it was not an emergency because the person only called once. If this rings true for you, begin to try this same process in other situations.

Each day you encounter people, places and things that make you smile or make you shudder. Make a mental note of each. List those things that resonate positively with your heart and list those that do not. Keep every enjoyable moment in your recipe!

"Time is the most valuable coin in your life. You and you alone determine how that coin will be spent. Be careful that you do not let others spend it for you."

Carl Sandburg

Your "awareness" meter is also a helpful tool for monitoring whether your words match your desires. What comes out of your mouth can have a unique influence on your every day experiences.

Have you ever been around a person that constantly dramatizes scenarios using terms like "It drives me crazy," "I'd die if," "to die for," "It kills me," "We can't afford," "I'm sick and tired of," "makes me sick," "scares me to death." Each of these negative statements should be more positively rephrased or avoided. Make it an exercise with a friend that when they catch you choosing negative words they ask you to restate them another way. You will both benefit.

This recently had an impact on me as I was taking my daily walk. A lady was taking her trash to the curb as I walked by her house. As I approached I said, "Good morning!" She replied, "I should be doing what you're doing. I've been sleeping in and it's killing me." I have been sensitive to people's choice of words for quite a long time, but this one takes the cake. How will her words affect her longevity?

"There is an old saying that man dares use his words for only three purposes, to heal, bless or prosper."

Frances Scovell Shinn

Don't be discouraged if others don't embrace your desire for personal development or show little interest in your newfound passion. Keep in mind that finding your authentic recipe will change your outlook and may confuse those who are unaware of how to improve their own lives. Protect your secret recipe and be leery of inexperienced cooks who feel the need to advise you about yours! Season your recipe to your own taste, without the influence of other's opinions and input. Combine only the ingredients that are true to your heart and refine your life recipe as new experiences and circumstances influence your palate!

"To accomplish great things, we must not only act, but also dream; not only plan, but also believe."

Anatole France

Are you ready to create your Recipe for Life?
We'll start with the spoon!

Chapter 2:
Use Your Spoon

Does your life lack excitement? Have you lost your enthusiasm for living?

When we keep making the same menu for dinner week after week, our taste buds become dulled. When life begins to follow the same monotonous course, we forget that we have the power to balance our lives, and bring back the excitement.

As an attempt to balance work and family, we often carry preprogrammed rules from childhood into our adult lives. This particular rule comes to mind: You can play outside when you finish your chores. The problem is our chores and to-do lists are ongoing and will never be completed. Small indulgences and rewards are necessary on a daily basis to help achieve balance.

For instance, if your job requires a tedious task like catching up on industry-related materials, perhaps it would be more enjoyable if you did this while enjoying a beverage at your favorite bookstore. If your errand list is overwhelming, catch up with a friend over coffee midway through the list. Even small pleasures can make us more effective and productive when they are blended with the simple demands of daily life.

Exercise #3: Daily Indulgences

Write down three ideas to add small indulgences to your daily routine. Be creative!

1.
2.
3.

That's why we called this chapter "Use Your Spoon." Life is a huge menu of choices. As you discover the ingredients that help you feel your best, your next challenge is to take action. When you come to a fork in the road, taste a spoonful of each option, find a good balance and trust your instincts.

A Spoonful of Balance

An important aspect of balance that is often neglected is choosing nutritious foods and exercising to gain greater mental alertness. Pairing this with adequate rest and relaxation will contribute to better mental and physical health. You will inevitably feel more alert, engaged, and empowered to accomplish goals and projects when you choose a healthy routine.

Once you begin selecting a diet of only nourishing and wholesome ingredients, anything less will seem like fodder. Becoming knowledgeable about healthy food ingredients and incorporating them into your diet will result in you feeling good and will eventually become a way of life. You may even find yourself scrutinizing restaurant menus to see what oils they use and whether they offer organic and vegetarian alternatives.

Fill your cupboards with healthy ingredients. Grocery stores are arranged with the fresh produce, fish, dairy and meat counters on the outside perimeter. The inside aisles contain the processed, refined and enriched products that typically have more artificial ingredients, preservatives and chemicals. Stay away from packaged foods loaded with unnatural ingredients!

"To be fully engaged, we must be physically energized, emotionally connected, mentally focused and spiritually aligned with a purpose beyond our immediate self-interest."

Jim Loeher

Seeking balance contributes to a more peaceful existence. Balance means knowing how to begin your day so that it will be the best it can be. Rather than jumping out of bed and rushing into the shower, I enjoy my cup of coffee in bed, reading or journaling for a few minutes to center myself.

The Center is the Creamiest, Meatiest & Tastiest Part

Allowing yourself some quiet time in the morning before you start your day can be rewarding. The practice of "getting centered" may include yoga, meditation, exercise or a personal routine that works for you.

A calm beginning to the day allows you to clear your mind and function at maximum capacity. Being solidly centered allows you to identify more opportunities that require careful maneuvering and clear decision-making throughout your day.

"It is well to be up before daybreak, for such habits contribute to health, wealth, and wisdom."

Aristotle

Your Brain and Your Face

Unexpected forks in the road may present opportunities to reassess and revamp your recipe. The job at the gourmet food store had a tremendous impact on my quality of life. While there, I discovered that my creative side that had been overshadowed by the highly analytical positions I kept pursuing. I now loved my time on the sales floor discussing food, wine and travel with customers. Work felt like play and set the stage for the transition to the culinary arts.

This stopover not only led me to write and publish a cookbook (with the help of a severance package from a second layoff), but also to teach cooking classes and discover my Recipe for Life.

The creativity and organization required for these projects exercised both the creative right side of my brain, and the analytical left side of my brain.

The brain needs exercise just like the muscles you use at the gym. If you only lifted weights to strengthen your right arm, your right arm muscles would be more defined while the left arm muscles would appear flabby in comparison. The same happens when you exercise one side of your brain more regularly. Your face can appear somewhat distorted.

Before I began exercising my creative outlet through cooking, the left side of my face was tired and sad looking. Your right brain, which is creative, controls the left side of your body. The analytical left side of the brain controls the right side of the body. The balance or lack of balance is revealed when you look at the each side of your face in a mirror. There may be distinct differences in your features in the left and right side of your face if you are not exercising both sides of your brain. You can even give yourself a facelift by balancing your left and right brain activities, but it is up to you to know what side of your brain is not being nurtured.

The self-expression I discovered through culinary instruction and writing made working enjoyable. When you discover a career, job or an interest that inspires or motivates you, it can serve as a tool to aging more gracefully. Your features soften and your appearance is enhanced with a newfound inner connection to purpose-driven work. We oftentimes discover how to create the lives we want when

RECIPE FOR LIFE

we discover the things that make us feel alive and connected to our core wants and needs.

Would rediscovering talents or interests you once had as a child improve your satisfaction? Is there an activity you enjoy where the hours fly by without noticing? These type of ingredients add depth and meaning to your Recipe for Life. The euphoric feelings that accompany these discoveries will improve your overall recipe.

"Man cannot discover new oceans unless he has the courage to lose sight of the shore."

André Gide

Select Your Ingredients

Try this exercise to help get you started on your recipe. Choose seven items that you need in order to feel fulfilled. Start with the foundation of good health - physical, mental and spiritual. Layer your choices in life to create an interesting, complex recipe unique to you.

Exercise #4: Seven Ingredients

1.
2.
3.
4.
5.
6.
7.

16

Today, commit to paper the list of ingredients for the Recipe for Life that works for you. (What makes you happy and content?) Then look at it daily so your desires and intentions remain in focus. Once your desires are outlined on the ingredient list, you can easily determine whether new ingredients fit your priorities, values and personal preferences. For example, we all know if we want to do the things we desire, we have to have a budget for them. A "Recipe on Budget" is your financial freedom. What does that mean to you? It could be an abundance of money to support your family's lifestyle. How much will you need to feel abundant?

Start with the necessities and move to the more frivolous things specific to you. Do you like to go out dancing? How often would you like to go? Check out the details of where you want to go and make a plan.

As you learn more about yourself, you will begin to make changes and adjust your recipe to be more specific or to set more focused goals. (Example: Start an automatic draft to put 10% of each paycheck into a separate account.) Keep your recipe list in a visible spot so that you can easily refer back to it when your life falls out of balance or becomes unmanageable!

Choosing from life's menu of choices is similar to ordering off of a restaurant menu. Focus on what you are hungry for in life instead of the empty calorie junk foods (time filling activities) that fill you up but leave you hungry for true nourishment derived from fulfilling dreams and desires. Continually feed and expand your mind by listening to music and tapes, attending workshops and seminars or reading. Introduce new topics into your world to see if they resonate with you. Clearly define the joys that inspire and invigorate you. Begin to clearly define your wants and needs in order to visualize and create a happy and satisfying life.

What does your ideal life look like? What steps can you take to get there?

"Begin each day, task, or project with a clear vision of your desired direction and destination, and then continue by flexing your proactive muscles to make things happen."

Stephen Covey

CHAPTER 3:
LIVE DELICIOUSLY

We live in a country that offers a world of cuisines. Like any restaurant menu, life also offers a plethora of choices.

If you ordered a distasteful entree off one of those menus, would you go back to that restaurant and order it again? Of course not, so why repeat patterns in your life that have been unsuccessful or unrewarding?

Have you ever attended an event where you felt uncomfortable? Maybe the vibe in the room was negative or you felt self-conscious among the crowd. Perhaps you cannot pinpoint the exact feeling, but the next time you get a similar invitation, you may reflect back on those feelings and choose not to attend.

The opposite is true when you choose to connect with people who share your vision. A spirited exchange conversing about dreams and desires can be exhilarating! People you connect with add complexity to your recipe. People who are like-minded or people you wish to emulate introduce new techniques, interesting perspectives and sometimes exotic twists to what may otherwise be a simple recipe.

Subtle inklings of discomfort or comfort in such situations are the result of listening to your body's reactions using your head, heart and gut. Some people react to these situations without relating them to the way their body feels. You should acknowledge whether a person or scenario drags you down and drains you or inspires you should be recognized. Take notice and seek to find more of the exciting scenarios that ignite your passion.

You'll find you have more time for yourself and those that encourage and support you if you follow the 80/20 rule. The rule states that 80% of your results come from 20% of your actions.

This works for your life recipe as well. Spend your time and energy on the top 20% of the people, projects and desires that matter most. If you try to placate everyone in your life and spread yourself too thin, then you will become frustrated and unlikely to be fulfilled. Make quality decisions of how and with whom you spend your time.

The 80/20 Rule

If you focus on doing the top 20% of anything right with concentrated effort, you will be on the right track. We oftentimes beat ourselves up with a new diet or regimen. If we take in to account the 80/20 rule, we allow moderation and a less stringent set of rules that are more easily accomplished. Taking the "right" action 20% of the time will reap 80% of the results. In other words, on your list of ten resolutions to lose weight, pick the top two to focus on. My first choice would be expend more calories than I eat, the other would be to exercise. These two things alone versus a list of ten, will help you accomplish your goals more quickly. You'll be encouraged by results.

Even if you turn your thoughts 20% of the time to the top actions to get results, you are more likely to receive them. What you focus on...expands. Focusing on the negative components of the world as well as the things we don't want in our lives may have something to do with the dis"ease" that plagues our world.

"Learn to keep the door shut, keep out of your mind, out of your office, and out of your world, every element that seeks admittance with no definite helpful end in view."

George Mathew Adams

To Be, or Not To Be

Sometimes, getting what you "don't want" in life often catapults you to look for what you "do want" because the pain or the discomfort can be uncomfortable or even unbearable. This applies to everything - spouses, jobs and a host of other things. Past mistakes are not necessarily errors, but may be great motivators to define and create a Recipe for Life that works for you. A bad choice may be just the experience you need at the time to decide what you do want. Recognize who you are NOT while on the way to becoming who you are.

Exercise #5: I Am, I Am Not

Imagine that you're redefining yourself. Write down seven traits that now describe you, and three that you no longer tolerate. For example, I am supportive of family members, but I am not tolerant of self-inflicted dysfunction. Consider your "I am" statements as affirmations of who you really are today. Some of the affirmations I include are: I am happy, I am creative, I am driven. It never hurts to begin your day reviewing your positive traits!

I AM:
1.
2.
3.
4.
5.
6.

I AM NOT:
1.
2.
3.

We are all guilty of the mind chatter or repetitious dialogue that plays in our head that repeats "I should have..." Albert Ellis popularized the phrase "Don't should on yourself."

Instead of punishing yourself for the past, focus on the things you would like to appear in your life like exciting opportunities and interesting people. Allow your newly acquired life lessons to propel you toward better choices and motivate you to attract more positive experiences and thoughts. Tolerate your past mistakes and construct the future carefully, personalizing the ideal recipe to suit you. Appreciate how far you have come and the lessons you have learned along the way! How does your recipe taste so far?

The words you choose can magnify situations if you choose to continually criticize, condemn and complain as Dale Carnegie suggested. I chose my personal three Cs highlighting the positive aspects of making Choices, Connecting, and Complimenting.

"Any fool can criticize, condemn, and complain, but it takes character and self-control to be understanding and forgiving."

Dale Carnegie

Choose!
Choose only what you want for your life recipe based on what you would like to create. Choosing includes deciding what invitations to accept, what friends to hang out with and what projects to pursue.

Sharing your heart's desires with another person and supporting each other's endeavors can be powerful.

Share your heart's deepest desires with someone. It's scary, but you'll feel the supercharged energy of two people exchanging thoughts. Your dreams won't feel so far out of reach when someone else is helping you reach for them! You'll be fully present – "living in the moment." Achieving this energy requires focusing on the people in your presence wholeheartedly. In all areas of your life, direct your thoughts and energy to the moment you are living and the people living it with you.

"As we let our own light shine, we unconsciously give other people permission to do the same. As we are liberated from our own fear, our presence automatically liberates others."

Marianne Williamson

Connect – without cables!

A neighborly, old-fashioned "hello" when someone passes by is no longer the norm. Our fast-paced plugged-in lifestyle has led to a deterioration of some of the common connections that used to vibrate within communities.

Connecting also means acknowledging others as you maneuver through your day. Look everyone in the eye. Learn a sales clerk's name at a store you frequent. Take time to get to know someone outside your department at work. Treat a new acquaintance to coffee. Everybody needs those small sweet connections!

By letting your own light shine, you give a glimpse of your personality to everyone you meet. Your friendly "hello" may be the one bright spot in a stranger's or friend's day.

My life has unfolded in interesting ways after having engaged in conversations with strangers. Several of these conversations have led me to extend an invitation to coffee or lunch. My Recipe for Life has been greatly enhanced by these chance meetings with acquaintances who later became friends.

"God works in unexpected places, through unexpected people, at unexpected times, His wonders to perform."

Florence Scovel Shinn

Give Compliments

The third C reaps great rewards for both the giver and the receiver. Sincere, timely compliments expressed to partners, co-workers and children for accomplishments, achievements and good deeds never go unnoticed.

Women seem to compliment one another on a regular basis. Great hair, cute shoes are in our regular vocabulary, but men don't hear this as often. Since complimenting comes natural to women, I feel strongly that we should use this gift in our relationships at home and in the workplace.

Encouraging words tend to make people want to repeat positive behavior in order to receive more praise. It is rare that anyone tires of compliments.

CHAPTER 4:
SHARE YOUR RECIPE

Did you set goals for what you wanted to accomplish by age 30? 40? 50? 60? If you are in the habit of making a to-do list every day, do you keep your dreams and desires high on your list?

The dreams we have, the desires that burn in our bellies, can propel us to action with fixed determination as long as we don't bury them amidst our to-do lists. Your base recipe should have a minimum of 7 things that keep you fulfilled, fueling the fire that keeps your passion ignited. If your current recipe is no longer igniting passion, perhaps you need to seek some more inspiring ingredients to stoke your fire.

When reviewing your current recipe, consider the areas of life that may need improvement. Evaluate your career, physical environment (home, city, and location), financial abundance, health, relationships, personal and spiritual growth, recreation and your contribution to your community. Small changes in one or many areas may yield big results and improve your recipe. When you change just a few things to be more of what you want from life, you change your destiny. It is also important to continue to shop for quality ingredients to add to your personal recipe.

"Growth, power, and wholeness are obtained only through self-knowledge, truthful expression, and the courage to act on what we know to be real within ourselves."

Marsha Sinetar

I have a collage of pictures that represent my ideal recipe glued to a poster board that I call my vision board. It is a collection of pictures and inspiring words from cooking, spiritual, and travel magazines. When a picture or message moves me, I cut it out. These pictures are glued to my poster board as a visual reminder to encourage me to dream and set goals for things I would like in my life.

Exercise #6: Vision Board

To create your own vision board, follow the diagram below. Choose pictures that inspire you to feel what it would be like if you were prosperous, or had the ideal career or love relationship. Once you have started the project, keep it prominently displayed in a location where you will see it daily. Add to it when you find additional pictures or words that help visualize your dreams and desires.

Your passions should ignite your recipe. When you look back on what memories evoke the most pleasant feelings, you may recognize a pattern that explains why you enjoy certain activities. I discovered that my time abroad during college is really where my appreciation of food began. Many of my college memories are of the meals I shared while traveling overseas with international colleagues. Had I been more tuned into my desires back then, I might have entered the culinary world much earlier in my career.

Wealth & Prosperity	Fame & Reputation	Love & Marriage
Family	Health	Creativity & Children
Knowledge & Self Cultivation	Career	Helpful People & Travel

Today, cooking for family and guests as well as teaching culinary classes and presenting Recipe for Life is very rewarding to me. We all possess unique talents that when shared with others give us a sense of fulfillment. Talents and passions add flavor to your recipe and allow you to share your gifts with others.

"Each of us is meant to have a character all our own, to be what no other can exactly be, do what no other can exactly do."

Channing

You are the chef of your own recipe so create a satisfying and fulfilling life. As you figure out your key ingredients, consider what would lead you closer to your dream life. Healthy relationships, financial abundance, and career aspirations are all part of a successful plan.

The list of ingredients and their proportions will fluctuate and change as your palate matures. As you age, new discoveries will enrich your overall recipe.

Your recipe and my recipe will be completely different because our tastes and needs differ. Here is a sample of my ingredients and what they represent in my life recipe.

Write Your Recipe for Life

Here's Mine:

1. "Meat of the Recipe" – Projects: a day that consists of writing, presentations and social media. Connecting with my "audience" and inspiring those around me to create their ideal Recipe for Life.

2. "Health of the Recipe" – Mental and Physical Well-being: eating nutritious foods, exercising regularly and sleeping 7 hours per night keeps me alert to new opportunities. Focusing on the good things that happen throughout the week keeps me positively motivated.

3. "Binder of the Recipe" – What holds a recipe together? Family: supportive with a mutual interest in each other's dreams and desires. This includes sharing quality time together-cooking and entertaining our friends and family.

4. "Spice in the Recipe" – Excitement: traveling and tasting the flavors of the world, golfing and enjoying music. Continue attending events in our city and community.

5. "A Recipe on Budget" – Financial Freedom: abundance of money to support our family's desired lifestyle. A recipe that smartly blends simplicity with extravagance to ensure long-term security.

6. "Complexity of the Recipe" – Network: a supportive, interesting, colorful and ever-expanding network of friends and business associates. Continued personal development and learning.

7. "A Nourishing Recipe" – Staying Grounded: centered and continually learning and evolving. Knowing my schedule limits and being at peace with my spiritual growth and overall well-being.

Exercise #7: Write Yours!
Meat:
Health:
Binder:
Spice:
Budget:
Complexity:
Nourishment:

Mixed in the proper proportions and adjusted as needed, this combination works well for me. What's yours? Write it down, taste it, try it for a few days, tweak, taste again. When you've found one you love, post it where it is visible and on our Facebook community (www.facebook.com/recipeforlife) to help you use it every day!

Your recipe may require more outdoor time, pampering and totally different adventures than I need. We will differ in our likes and dislikes. Husbands and wives may have completely different recipe ingredients, but the blending of the two may complement one another and create a harmonious relationship. I highly recommend everyone have their own individual recipe or you may become part of someone else's recipe. When that occurs, life can seem unsatisfying and you may not understand the reasons why.

"Life begins at the end of your comfort zone."

Neale Donald Walsch

Life is a huge menu of choices. It's overwhelming at times. Discover the ingredients that give <u>you</u> the most joy and pleasure. Create your own Recipe for Life to follow every day. When you come to a fork in the road, you'll know exactly which way to go.

Plan for your life like you would a celebration. Stimulate all of your senses. Pay close attention to the details and keep your guest list interesting!

Remember your new ABC's of the Recipe for Life. Start by becoming "aware" of how your decisions "feel" when choosing your recipe ingredients. Find a "balance" of physical and mental existence so it is easier to recognize opportunities and lifestyle improvements. Learn to establish meaningful "connections" with others and "choose" only what YOU want to add to the recipe. Reach for your "dreams" and fulfill your "desires". If you select the most favorable ingredients and people for your unique life recipe, your life will sizzle with satisfaction.

"Destiny is not a matter of chance, it is a matter of choice; it is not a thing to be waited for, it is a thing to be achieved."

Winston Churchill

Thank you for reading and participating in Recipe for Life! The greatest joys of your life are ahead – and I hope your recipe helps you seize and savor all the delicious moments that life has to offer.

Any time you need support, guidance, or dinner ideas, contact me via my blog (www.recipeforlife. biz), email (Debbie@recipeforlife.biz) or Twitter (@recipeforlife).

I also give presentations to companies and organizations who desire a less stressful, more productive work-life balance. We do new exercises to help people prioritize their goals, improve health and well-being to initiate positive life changes. I'd love to speak to your group. Give me a call and I can customize a program for you.

Phone: 817.329.8538.

Bon appétit my friends – and keep your fork! There is a bonus chapter on Superfoods and a chapter of recipes utilizing the superfoods!

CHAPTER 5:
ICING ON THE CAKE

Building your life recipe is an important part of becoming fulfilled and satisfied every day, but it cannot happen if you feel lousy. By changing what you eat, you can improve your health and begin to see results. You may lose a few pounds, feel more energized or both! One type diet does not work for everyone, but I have always felt the less manipulated by science it is, the better it is.

"As for butter versus margarine, I trust cows more than chemists."

Joan Gussow

In this chapter I have included the tips about the foods I feed my family and in Chapter 6 are the recipes utilizing these superfoods.

Being a downright ambitious "foodie" you can bet that I will put satiety and taste high on the list and couple it with nutrition. Having healthy foods available and knowing what to do with them is also very important. If you have a package of Girl Scout Cookies sitting on the counter and nothing healthy in the fridge, the tendency is to opt for convenience. So, organization in shopping for healthy options will help you make better choices. With knowledge of the things that are good for you, a healthier lifestyle becomes more manageable.

Everything in moderation, as we have all been taught, actually works. That includes work and high stress activities, too. If stress is the antithesis of pleasure, then it follows that pleasure is the antithesis of stress. And the best way to fight stress, say researchers, Charnetski and Brennan, is with pleasure. Our bodies secrete chemicals called endorphins when we experience pleasure. Pleasure inducing experiences have been scientifically proven to promote health and well-being, like music, touch, pets, humor, positive attitude and insight.

"Feel-good pleasure is generally sensation-based: the taste of delicious food, the feel of silk, the luxury of a deep tissue shoulder rub, the beauty of an attractive image. Value-based pleasure, is derived from the sense that our lives are meaningful and have a higher purpose — that we have challenged ourselves to accomplish an important goal

ICING ON THE CAKE

or demonstrated a commitment or connection to something that matters to us. Both types of pleasure result in benefits for health and happiness."

William McDougal, psychologist

The taste of delicious food is key and with these superfoods recipes, you'll prepare not just delicious food, but healthy, delicious food. Superfoods provide nutrients and antioxidants that fight free radicals in the environment and help prevent cancer. The free radicals include: air pollution, pesticides, sunlight, tobacco smoke, drugs and even fried foods.

Below are the foods that can contribute to better health when they are consistently included in your weekly meal planning.

Love the Superfoods!

Blueberries: Ounce for ounce, blueberries provide more antioxidants than any other fruit. Antioxidants are good for fighting stress and help growth and repair of tissues and cells. Blueberries are a good source of vitamins A, C and E, beta-carotene and also a source of the minerals potassium, magnesium and fiber. Eating a diet rich in deep pigment from fruits and vegetables can preserve the brain machinery and boost the potency of neuron signals.

Black beans: Contain folate and thiamine as well as the minerals magnesium, iron and potassium. Full of fiber and protein, black beans help reduce blood cholesterol and stabilize blood sugar levels.

37

Broccoli: Broccoli contains properties that help detoxify pollutants, plus contains beta-carotene that helps with eyesight. It is full of fiber and vitamins A, C, K, beta-carotene and folate plus the minerals potassium and phosphorus.

Sweet Potatoes: Sweet potatoes contain fiber, vitamin C, E, beta-carotene, folate, thiamin and riboflavin. They also contain copper, magnesium, manganese, phosphorus and potassium.

Wild Salmon: Salmon contains omega 3-fatty acids that reduces the risk of heart disease by lowering triglycerides, "bad" cholesterol and blood pressure as well. Salmon also contains vitamins A, B6 and B12 vitamins as well as potassium, phosphorus and selenium.

Spinach: Folate in spinach helps prevent cancer. Vitamins in spinach include C, K, beta-carotene, thiamine and riboflavin and minerals include iron, calcium, potassium and zinc.

Tomatoes: Tomatoes contain vitamins A and C. They also contain the mineral potassium. Tomatoes provide fiber and the antioxidant carotenoid, which is believed to protect against cancer, heart disease and deterioration of eyesight in the aging.

Walnuts: A source of vitamin E, folate, thiamin and riboflavin. Walnuts also contain the minerals magnesium and potassium. This is the only nut that contains a significant amount of ellagic acid that is a cancer-fighting antioxidant. Walnuts also contain omega-3 fatty acids and contain polyunsaturated fats that reduce the bad cholesterol and increase the HDL "good" cholesterol.

Cruciferous vegetables: This is a scientific name for a group of vegetables that research has proven may provide protection against certain cancers. These vegetables which are all high in fiber, vitamins and minerals, are: broccoli, Brussels sprouts, cabbage, cauliflower, chard, kale, mustard greens, rutabagas and turnips.

Turkey Breast: Lean protein is good for you. Skinless turkey breast is one of the best.

Oranges: The most readily available source of vitamin C, which in turns lowers the rate of most causes of deaths in this country, such as, heart disease and cancer.

Pumpkin: Loaded with phytonutrients, it keeps our skin young and helps prevent damage from sunlight.

Steel Cut Oats: A surefire way to lower cholesterol.

"An ounce of prevention is worth a pound of cure."

Ben Franklin

Chapter 6:
A Gift for You
(Superfoods Recipes)

Blueberry Pomegranate Smoothie

Makes: 2 drinks

In a blender combine:

1 3/4	cups organic frozen blueberries
1 1/3	cups pomegranate juice
2	frozen strawberries

Pulse to blend to smooth consistency. Add water if needed. The drink should be pourable.

Blanched Asparagus with Wasabi Mayonnaise

Serves: 8

2 tablespoons, plus 2 teaspoons wasabi powder
1 tablespoon fresh squeezed lemon juice
1 tablespoon water
1 cup mayonnaise (light may be used)
2 bunches thin asparagus, trimmed

Blend the first four ingredients with a whisk. Cover and chill until ready to serve. Boil water and add asparagus. Boil approximately 3 minutes, depending on the size of the asparagus. Remove with tongs and place in ice water, to stop the cooking (called blanching). Serve with wasabi mayonnaise.

Goat Cheese Stuffed Zucchini
Serves: 6

3	(1 1/2 inch diameter) zucchini, halved lengthwise
1	teaspoon extra-virgin olive oil
1	tablespoon unsalted butter
2	garlic cloves, minced
5	ounces goat cheese
1/4	cup roasted red peppers, diced
1	teaspoon dried oregano
1/4	teaspoon ground black pepper
2	tablespoons minced fresh chives
1/4	teaspoon paprika
3	large leaves fresh basil, chiffonade

Preheat oven to 350°F. With a spoon, scrape the majority of the seeds from the zucchini. Place in a baking dish meat side up and drizzle with olive oil. Bake 20 minutes and remove from oven. Allow to cool to room temperature. Add the butter to a small sauté pan and sauté the garlic until fragrant, but not browned approximately 2 to 3 minutes. With the back of a spoon, mash the goat cheese with the garlic, peppers, oregano, pepper and chives. Cut the zucchini in 3/4-inch pieces and stuff evenly with the goat cheese (or use a pastry bag and star tip to pipe into zucchini). Sprinkle with paprika and fresh basil and serve.

Note: Chiffonade means to stack the basil leaves, roll and cut into thin strips.

Shrimp and Hearts of Palm Salad
Serves: 6

1/2	pound shrimp (21/25 count), shelled and deveined
4	cups water
1	bay leaf
12	allspice berries
	Zest of 1/2 lime
2	teaspoons sea salt

Salad

1	small red onion, thinly sliced
2	medium ripe tomatoes, seeded and cut in 1/4-inch cubes
8	ounces or 4 hearts of palm, cut in 1/2-inch rounds

Dressing

1/2	cup extra virgin olive oil
1	tablespoon white balsamic vinegar
1	tablespoon fresh orange juice
1/2	teaspoon sea salt
	Pinch cumin
1/2	seeded minced jalapeno
1	tablespoon finely chopped cilantro

Bring the water to boil over medium heat and add the next four ingredients. Add the shrimp and cook until slightly coiled (about 3 minutes). Remove shrimp with a slotted spoon and put shrimp in ice water. Drain shrimp and add to bowl with onion and tomato. In a bowl, whisk oil, vinegar and remaining ingredients together. Pour over shrimp mixture and toss to combine. Serve just after making or chilled on a lettuce leaf. A nice light dinner or side salad!

Asian Broccoli Almond Slaw

Serves: 8

1	head Napa cabbage
1	bunch (6) green onions, chopped
3/4	cup raisins
1/2	cup canned black beans, rinsed and drained
1	cup sliced or slivered, toasted almonds
2	broccoli crowns

Dressing

1/2	cup grapeseed oil
1/2	cup honey
1/4	cup tarragon vinegar
1	tablespoon less-sodium soy sauce

Preheat oven to 350°F. Chop the cabbage (using about 2/3 of the cabbage-throw out tough white core), add onions and chill until ready to serve. Toast the almonds (approximately 4 minutes in the oven). Chop the top of the broccoli crown very fine. Just before serving, add the raisins, black beans, almonds and broccoli crown. Toss desired amount dressing with the salad ingredients. Refrigerate left-over dressing.

Asian Coleslaw with Peanut Dressing
Serves: 4
Dressing
>1/4 cup bottled Thai peanut sauce (such as House of Tsang)
>
>1/4 cup mayonnaise (light may be used)

Salad
>1 (14-ounce) bag coleslaw
>
>1/2 cup diced red pepper (1/4-inch pieces)
>
>3 large green onions, minced (white and pale green parts only)

In a bowl, whisk the peanut sauce and mayonnaise together. Combine salad ingredients in a large bowl and toss with the dressing. Chill two hours to blend flavors or serve immediately, if desired.

Variations:

- *For a tasty main course, add 4 grilled turkey breasts (2 pounds)*
- *Add a can of organic black beans rinsed and drained*

Balsamic Maple Vinaigrette
Servings: 8

3	tablespoons balsamic vinegar
2	tablespoons pure maple syrup
1	small shallot, finely chopped (about 2 tablespoons)
2/3	cup extra virgin olive oil
1/8	teaspoon sea salt
1/4	teaspoon pepper
	Freshly ground pepper, to taste

To make the vinaigrette, mix all the ingredients in a jar with a tight fitting lid and shake vigorously. This vinaigrette is a perfect accompaniment to fresh spinach salad. Dress your favorite spinach salad and place the leftover vinaigrette in the refrigerator. Spinach can replace lettuce in any salad for a more nutritious accompaniment! Add candied walnuts, fried, crumbled bacon (nitrate free), Craisins and blue cheese, if desired.

Candied Walnuts

Servings: 8

3	cups walnut halves
2	tablespoons pure maple syrup
1	tablespoon extra virgin olive oil
1/8	teaspoon cayenne pepper (optional)
	Sea salt
	Ground black pepper

Preheat the oven to 350°F. In a large bowl, toss the walnuts with the maple syrup and olive oil. Sprinkle with cayenne if desired and a light sprinkle of salt and pepper. Toss together and evenly spread on lightly greased jelly roll pan. Bake at 350°F for 15 minutes. Good as a snack with wine or on salads (coarsely chopped).

Spinach Salad with Prosciutto and Capers
Serves: 4
Spinach Salad
1 (9-ounce) bag baby spinach
4 thin slices prosciutto, finely chopped
2 hard-boiled eggs, grated
2 tablespoons capers, drained and rinsed
2 tablespoons minced cornichons
2 tablespoons chopped fresh chives
6 cherry tomatoes, quartered

Lemon Dressing:
1 1/2 tablespoons freshly squeezed lemon juice (juice from 1/2 medium lemon)
1/2 teaspoon sea salt
1/4 teaspoon black pepper
3 tablespoons extra virgin olive oil
1 garlic clove, minced or pressed

Place the spinach (or arugula) in a large bowl. Add the prosciutto and the hard-boiled eggs. Set aside. In a separate bowl, make the dressing by mixing all the ingredients together. Add the remaining ingredients to the greens. Toss with desired amount of dressing. Refrigerate leftover dressing.

Note: Cornichons is French for "gherkins." They are crisp, tart pickles made from tiny cucumbers. Prosciutto is easy to chop using kitchen shears.

Broccoli Salad with Citrus Dressing
Serves: 6

Vinaigrette
- 1/2 cup fresh orange juice
- 1/4 cup fresh lemon juice
- 1 tablespoon honey
- 1 teaspoon fresh minced ginger

Salad
- 1 head broccoli tops, coarsely chopped (about 3 cups)
- 1 (15-ounce) can black beans, rinsed
- 1/3 cup finely diced red onion
- 1 cup chopped candied walnuts
- 1/2 cup dried cranberries (Craisins)

Candied Walnuts
- 3 cups walnut halves
- 2 tablespoons pure maple syrup
- 1 tablespoon extra virgin olive oil
- 1/8 teaspoon cayenne pepper (optional)
  - Sea salt, to taste
  - Ground black pepper, to taste

Preheat the oven to 350°F. In a large bowl, toss the walnuts with the maple syrup and olive oil. Sprinkle with cayenne if desired and a light sprinkle of salt and pepper. Toss together and evenly spread on lightly greased jelly roll pan. Bake at 350°F for

15 minutes. Chop the cup of walnuts for the salad and place remainder in an airtight container once cooled. Toss the salad ingredients together excluding the walnuts; add the dressing and refrigerate overnight. Add the walnuts just before serving.

Quinoa with Dates and Almonds

Serves: 8

2	cups water
1	cup quinoa (a great source of protein!)
1/2	teaspoon sea salt
1/3	cup chopped pitted dates
1/2	cup slivered or sliced almonds, toasted
1/2	cup minced fresh cilantro
1/4	cup minced green onions
	Sea salt, to tastes
	Ground black pepper, to taste

Dressing

1/4	cup extra virgin olive oil
1 1/2	tablespoons fresh lemon juice
1/4	teaspoon ground cardamom

Rinse the quinoa thoroughly according to package directions. Bring water to boil in medium saucepan. Add quinoa; stir and bring to boil. Cover and reduce heat to low and simmer approximately 20 minutes until water is absorbed. Remove from heat. Cover and let stand 5 minutes. Fluff with fork. Transfer to large bowl to cool. Whisk olive oil, lemon juice and cardamom to blend in small bowl. Drizzle over couscous. Mix in dates, almonds, minced cilantro, and green onions. Toss gently to blend ingredients and season to taste. May be served warm or at room temperature. Flavors will blend better if it stands at room temperature at least 1 hour before serving.

Note: This salad is a nice accompaniment to the Salmon with Mango and Dried Cherries.

Mediterranean Spinach Salad
Serves: 8
Salad

1	pint cherry or grape tomatoes, cut in half lengthwise
2	tablespoon fresh basil, cut in thin strips (chiffonade)
1/3	cup diced red onions
1	(14-ounce) can of hearts of palm, drained and sliced
6	ounces baby spinach leaves
1/2	red pepper, diced
4	stalks hearts of palm, drained and sliced
1/2	cup crumbled feta

Lemon Dressing

2	tablespoons lemon juice
1/2	teaspoon dried oregano
2	cloves garlic, minced or pressed
1/4	teaspoon pepper
1/4	teaspoon sea salt
1/3	cup extra virgin olive oil

For the dressing, mix the lemon juice with the next four ingredients. While whisking, slowly drizzle the olive oil into the mixture to emulsify. Gently toss the salad ingredients excluding feta. Gently fold the feta in with the tomatoes or crumble over the top of each serving. Keep leftover dressing refrigerated.

Artichoke Turkey Salad
Serves: 8

2/3	cup pecans
2	cups poached turkey cutlets (approximately 3 cutlets)
1/4	cup celery
1/4	cup onion
2	peppercorns
1	(14-ounce) can artichoke hearts, drained and finely chopped
3	tablespoons mayonnaise (light may be used)
3	tablespoons sour cream
1/4	cup minced green onion (white and pale green part only)
1	garlic clove, minced or pressed
1/2	teaspoon salt
1/2	teaspoon pepper
	Fresh parsley, minced

Preheat the oven to 350°F to toast the pecans, or toast them in a medium skillet turning frequently to prevent burning for approximately 4 minutes. To poach cutlets place turkey cutlets, onion, celery, and peppercorns in a skillet. Pour in enough boiling water to just cover the turkey. Cover and poach turkey over low heat for about 10 minutes or until turkey is fully cooked. Remove from pan and dice into bite-size pieces. (This can be done the night before. Chill until ready to use.) Just before serving, mix with the mayonnaise, sour cream, onion, garlic and salt and pepper. Blend the turkey with artichokes and coat with the mayonnaise mixture. Garnish with minced parsley.

Turmeric Turkey Salad
Serves: 6

6	boneless, skinless turkey breasts
1	tablespoon lime juice
1	teaspoon coriander
1	teaspoon sea salt
1/2	teaspoon ginger
1/2	teaspoon turmeric
1/4	teaspoon cinnamon
1/2	teaspoon pepper
1	tablespoon olive oil
1	(9-ounce) bag baby spinach
1/3	cup dried cranberries (Craisins) or raisins
1/3	cup sliced red onion
1/3	cup walnuts
1/3	crumbled feta or blue cheese

Mix the lime juice with the spices and marinate 20 minutes at room temperature. In a skillet, heat the olive oil and sauté the turkey approximately 3 minutes a side. Set aside to cool slightly. Cut in small pieces. Place the Bragg's vinaigrette ingredients in a canning jar and shake to blend. Mix baby spinach with remaining ingredients. Toss with desired amount dressing. Refrigerate leftover dressing.

Bragg's Cider Vinaigrette
Serves: 8

3	tablespoons Bragg's apple cider vinegar
1	teaspoon Dijon mustard
1/3	extra virgin olive oil
1	tablespoon pure maple syrup

Broccoli Soup
Serves: 6

1	teaspoon olive oil
3	medium cloves garlic
2	medium leeks, cleaned and sliced (white and pale green part only)
3	stalks celery, chopped
1	small carrot, peeled and chopped
1	pound broccoli tops, chopped
7	cups vegetable or chicken broth or stock
1	cup fresh basil leaves
	Sea salt, to taste
	Ground black pepper, to taste
1/2	cup heavy cream (optional)

In a large soup pot, heat the oil and sauté the garlic until softened, but not browned. Add the leeks, celery carrot, broccoli and broth. Cover and cook 10 to 15 minutes or until carrot is soft. Turn off heat and add basil, allow to wilt (keep lid on). In batches, place soup ingredients in blender and puree. Pour back in soup pot to heat slightly and add cream if desired.

Roasted Pumpkin Soup

Serves: 6

4	tablespoons butter, divided use
1	2 3/4 pound pumpkin, peeled, diced, seeds removed
1	cup diced yellow onion
1	garlic clove, peeled
1	cup peeled, diced red pepper, seeds and stem removed
1	celery stalk, peeled and sliced
1	tablespoon, peeled, sliced fresh ginger
1	small dried red chile
1/4	teaspoon Madras curry powder
1	teaspoon paprika
4	cups chicken stock
3/4	cup heavy cream
	Sea salt, to taste
	Ground white pepper, to taste
1/2	cup fresh cilantro, stems removed, chopped

Butter a 9 x 13-inch glass baking dish. Preheat the oven to 400°F. Place the remaining butter, pumpkin, vegetables, spices and broth in the dish. Cover with foil and roast until tender approximately 40 to 60 minutes. In a powerful blender, such as a Vita-Mix, puree the mixture until smooth. Return soup to a saucepan and add cream. Reheat before serving. Add salt and white pepper. Garnish individual servings with cilantro and serve.

Note: Use a vegetable peeler to remove the shiny skin from the outside of the red pepper and the strings on the celery for a smoother texture soup.

Orange Roughy with Artichokes

Serves: 4

Fish

- 1 tablespoon minced parsley
- 2 tablespoons chopped fresh thyme
- 2 tablespoons chopped fresh oregano
- 4 orange roughy or other white fish fillets (approximately 2 pounds)
- 2 tablespoons freshly squeezed lemon juice

Artichoke Butter Sauce

- 2 tablespoons butter
- 2 tablespoons flour
- 1 cup chicken or vegetable broth or stock
  Pinch ground nutmeg
- 1 (14-ounce) can artichokes, drained and chopped
- 1/4 teaspoon sea salt
- 1/8 teaspoon pepper
  Chopped parsley for garnish

Preheat the oven to 350°F. Mix the herbs together. Brush the fillets of fish with lemon and let sit for 10 minutes, and then roll in herbs. Bake the fish for approximately 18 to 20 minutes until no longer opaque. While the fish is baking, make the sauce. Heat butter until melted and stir in the flour. Add the broth and bring to boil stirring constantly with a whisk. As mixture begins to thicken, add nutmeg and artichokes. Add salt and pepper. Serve over herbed fish. Garnish with parsley.

Note: If dried herbs are used then use only 1/3 of the measurement for each.

Fish with Okra and Tomatoes

Serves: 4

1	teaspoon freshly squeezed lemon juice
4	white fish fillets (approximately 1 pound), cut into 1 1/4-inch-wide strips
1	tablespoon cold, unsalted butter
1	tablespoon olive oil
1/2	cup coarsely chopped pecans
1	bunch green onions (5-6 small), chopped (white and pale green part)
	Black pepper, to taste
1	(16-ounce) package frozen okra (sliced)
3	plum tomatoes, seeded and diced
1/2	teaspoon sea salt (optional)
	Cooked brown rice

Sprinkle lemon over the fish and let sit 10 minutes. Heat 1/2 tablespoon butter in a small skillet and toast the pecans over medium heat until fragrant (about 3 to 4 minutes) and set aside. In a large skillet, heat the olive oil. Cook green onions until translucent. Add the pepper, okra and tomatoes. Cook until okra softens and liquid boils. Add the fish, salt and remaining butter. Gently toss the fish in the liquid until no longer opaque. Spoon rice onto plates and top with fish mixture; sprinkle with toasted pecans.

Salmon with Fresh Vegetables and Ginger
Serves: 4

2	tablespoons unsalted butter, divided use
1	tablespoon olive oil
4	(8-ounce) wild salmon fillets
1	tablespoon turbinado or raw sugar
1/2	cup walnuts
2/3	cup broth or bouillon (chicken or lobster)
1/3	cup orange juice
1	tablespoon less-sodium soy sauce
1	tablespoon cornstarch
1	tablespoon garlic
1	tablespoon fresh minced ginger
1/8	teaspoon white pepper
1	cup carrot or sweet potato, peeled and julienne
1	red pepper, thinly sliced
1 1/2	cups broccoli florets
2	green onions, sliced on diagonal (white and pale green only)
1/2	cup fresh spinach leaves
	Cooked brown rice

Heat the oven to 150°F. In a skillet, heat one tablespoon of butter with teaspoon oil and cook the salmon skin side down. Cook approximately 4 minutes per side until slightly golden and cooked through (pink throughout). Transfer salmon to an ovenproof platter and place in oven to keep warm. Clean the pan, removing any skin that stuck to the bottom to use for the sauce and vegetables. With a paper towel, coat a small pan with remaining butter and melt the sugar. Add the walnuts and toast in the sugar to coat and caramelize. Remove nuts onto a piece of wax paper. In a small glass bowl, mix the broth, soy sauce, cornstarch and sugar together. Heat the olive oil over medium high heat and sauté the garlic and ginger. Add the pepper and sweet potatoes, simmer with lid on over low 3 minutes. Begin adding the broccoli, pepper onion and again simmer with the lid on 3 minutes. As the broccoli begins to get tender (usually at about 9 minutes of cook time), add the spinach. Add the broth mixture and bring to boil to thicken. Add the salmon back into the pan. Serve the salmon and vegetables over the cooked brown rice.

Salmon Baked in Parchment

Serves:

2   (8-ounce) wild salmon fillets
8   paper thin slices sweet potato
2   tablespoons chopped walnuts
2   green onions (white and pale green)
1   cup spinach leaves
1   teaspoon fresh minced ginger
1   teaspoon fresh minced garlic
1   tablespoon pure maple syrup

Preheat the oven to 350°F. Begin by cutting four pieces parchment into squares of 8 x 8-inches so you have a top and a bottom for each piece of fish. Place a piece of fish on two pieces of parchment, reserving the other pieces for the top. Layer the sweet potatoes, walnuts, onion and spinach evenly over the two fish pieces. Sprinkle with the garlic, ginger and syrup. Cover the fish with other piece parchment and crimp the edges to make two enclosed packets of fish to bake. Bake 15 to 18 minutes on a sheet pan.

Salmon with Mango and Dried Cherries

Serves: 4

3	tablespoons turbinado or raw brown sugar
1/4	teaspoon ground black pepper
4	(8-ounce) wild salmon fillets
1	tablespoon butter
1	teaspoon extra virgin olive oil
1	ripe mango peeled, pitted and diced
1/2	cup dried Bing or tart cherries (if large, cut in half)
2	teaspoons white balsamic vinegar
1/4	teaspoon red pepper flakes (optional)
1/4	cup white wine

Heat the oven to 150°F. Mix the brown sugar and black pepper. Rub the mixture over the fish. Heat the butter and oil in a large sauté pan medium heat and add salmon. Cook the salmon approximately 4 minutes per side or until slightly golden and cooked through (pink throughout). Transfer salmon to an ovenproof platter and place in oven to keep warm. Add the mango, cherries, balsamic, red pepper flakes and wine to the skillet to heat over medium heat approximately 5 minutes. Remove fish from oven. Serve the fish drizzled with the mango-cherry mixture.

Note: Cooked brown rice or the Quinoa with Dates and Almonds are wonderful with this dish.

Salmon with Mustard Cream
Serves: 4

- 2 tablespoons unsalted butter
- 1 teaspoon extra-virgin olive oil
- 4 (8-ounce) wild salmon fillets
- 1/4 teaspoon dried thyme leaves
- 1/4 teaspoon ground black pepper

Mustard Cream

- 3/4 cup chicken broth or stock
- 4 1/2 teaspoons coarse-grained Dijon mustard
- 2 tablespoons heavy cream
- 1 tablespoon cornstarch (optional)
  Cooked brown rice

Heat the butter and oil in a large skillet or sauté pan. Sprinkle salmon with thyme and pepper. Place salmon skin side down. Cook the salmon 4 minutes per side. Remove the skin. (Skin should remove easily.) Transfer the cooked salmon to an ovenproof platter or baking dish and place in a 150°F oven while you make the sauce. In the same skillet bring the chicken stock to boil. Add the mustard and cream and bring to boil, whisking to blend. If the mixture is not to your desired thickness, a mixture of equal parts of cornstarch and cold water (approximately one tablespoon of each) and add just a bit to the boiling mixture while whisking. Repeat if necessary to get desired thickness. Serve salmon over the rice drizzled with the sauce.

Salmon with Honey-Soy Sauce

Serves: 4

2	tablespoons honey
2	tablespoons less-sodium soy sauce
2	teaspoons Dijon mustard
2	tablespoons butter, divided use
1	teaspoon extra virgin olive oil
4	(8-ounce) wild salmon fillets
2	cups portobello mushrooms
2	cloves garlic, minced
2	tablespoons (1/4 stick) unsalted butter
2	tablespoons dry white wine
2	green onions, sliced diagonally into 1/4-inch pieces
	Cooked brown rice

Preheat oven to 350°F. In a small bowl, whisk together honey, soy sauce and mustard and set aside. Melt a tablespoon butter and oil in a large skillet over medium heat and add the salmon fillets, skin side down. Cook the salmon 4 minutes per side. Remove the skin. (Skin should remove easily.) Transfer the cooked salmon to an ovenproof platter or baking dish and place in a 150°F oven while you make the sauce. Melt remaining butter and add the mushrooms and garlic. Sauté to soften mushrooms. Add the wine to the hot skillet and deglaze the pan scraping all the bits with a spatula. Add the honey mixture to the skillet and boil for 1 minute. Stir the green onions into the sauce just before serving and pour over the cooked salmon.

Salmon with Brown Butter Sauce

Serves: 4

2 tablespoons unsalted butter
2 tablespoons balsamic vinegar
1 tablespoon honey
1 tablespoon Dijon mustard
1 tablespoon extra virgin olive oil
4 (8-ounce) wild salmon fillets
1 tablespoon capers, drained and rinsed
1 medium tomato, seeded and diced (1/4-inch pieces)
Cooked brown rice

Melt butter in a saucepan over medium heat, swirling the pan occasionally, until butter is golden brown about 4 minutes. Remove from heat and add vinegar, honey and mustard. (Have a lid ready to cover pan otherwise vinegar will splatter when added to the hot butter.) In a large skillet, heat the olive oil and sauté fish skin side down until pink, approximately 4 minutes per side. (Skin should remove easily.) Warm the sauce and pour over the fish. Sprinkle with capers and tomatoes. Serve over rice.

Red Snapper with Garlic Lime Butter
Serves: 2

- 2 fillets skinless red snapper
- 6 tablespoons clarified butter
  Tony Chachere's Creole Seasoning, to taste
  Rice flour
- 1 teaspoon olive oil
- 3 medium garlic cloves, minced
- 2 tablespoons freshly squeezed lime juice (juice from 1 medium lime)

Have the butcher remove the skin from the fish when purchasing. Melt the butter in a saucepan. To clarify the butter, turn off heat and use a spoon to scrape the white foam off the top. Leave the solids from the bottom and pour the clarified butter in a skillet large enough to sauté the fillets. Sprinkle fillets with *Tony Chachere's* seasoning. Dust fillets with flour. Add the olive oil to the butter and increase heat to sauté garlic until just golden, but not browned. Add the fish to the pan and sauté until golden, approximately 10 minutes total, or until the fish is no longer opaque and is flaky. Remove the fillets from the pan and squeeze the lime juice into the butter. Pour the lime butter over the fish and serve hot.

Tuna Kebabs with Red Pepper Relish

Serves 8

2	pounds tuna steak, cut into 1-inch squares
3/4	cup red pepper jelly
2/3	cup spicy brown mustard
1/4	cup red wine vinegar
1	teaspoon ground black pepper
1/2	teaspoon sea salt
2	red bell peppers, minced
2	green onions, minced (white and pale green part only)
2	oranges, cut in 1-inch pieces
2	green bell peppers, cut into 1-inch pieces

If you are using wood skewers, soak the skewers in water for a 1/2 hour. Put the tuna in a large re-sealable plastic bag. Combine the jelly, mustard, vinegar, black pepper and salt in a glass bowl or measuring cup. Pour 1 cup of the marinade over the tuna. Seal the bag and refrigerate for 15 minutes. Combine the remaining marinade with the red pepper and onion in a serving bowl. (This will be the sauce you serve with the fish. Warm over low heat, if desired.) Once marinated, thread the tuna on the metal or wood skewers, alternating the tuna, orange pieces and green pepper (reserve excess marinade). Grill over medium-low heat approximately 8 to 10 minutes. Tuna will be slightly opaque. Baste halfway through cooking with the marinade. Serve the tuna skewers with the sauce.

Note: Serve rice and a salad for a beautiful balance of color and flavor.

Orange Roughy with Parmesan and Green Onions
Serves: 2

1 1/2	pounds skinless orange roughy fillets
1/4	cup (1/2 stick) butter, softened, divided use
2	tablespoons freshly squeezed lemon juice (juice from 1 medium lemon)
1/2	cup freshly grated Parmigiano-Reggiano cheese
3	tablespoons mayonnaise (light may be used)
3	tablespoons finely chopped green onion Dash of Tabasco red pepper sauce

Arrange your oven rack to be 4 inches from the broiler. Preheat the broiler. Place fillets in a buttered 9 x 13-inch glass baking dish; brush the fish with the lemon juice and let sit 10 minutes. Broil the fish until it is predominately white and flaky and no longer opaque. Combine the remaining ingredients in a bowl. Spread the mixture evenly over the fillets. Broil 2 to 3 minutes longer until topping is golden.

Variations: Fresh herbs (oregano, basil and thyme) may be added into the mixture for another variation of this recipe. Tilapia and other similar textured white fish may be substituted in place of roughy.

Orange Roughy with Tomatoes and Capers
Serves: 4

- 4   (8-ounce) orange roughy fillets
  Coarse sea salt
- 1/2 teaspoon ground white pepper, divided
- 2   tablespoons olive oil
- 1/4 cup dry white wine
- 2   tablespoons freshly squeezed lemon juice
  (juice from 1 medium lemon)
- 2   tablespoons cold unsalted butter, cut into
  chunks
- 6   green onions, sliced diagonally into
  1/4-inch pieces
- 1   tablespoon capers, drained and rinsed
- 1   large tomato, seeded and chopped
  (1/4-inch pieces)

Preheat the oven to 150°F. Season both sides of the fish with salt and a sprinkle of white pepper. Heat the olive oil in a large pan over medium heat. Cook the seasoned fish on each side for 4 minutes or until lightly browned. Remove the fish from the pan and place in ovenproof dish in the oven. To make the sauce, heat the wine and lemon juice in the pan the fish was sautéed in. Bring to a boil and let the mixture reduce by half; add cold butter and stir until melted. Add the onion, capers and tomatoes to the thickened sauce (cold butter thickens sauce) and cook for one minute. Remove the warm fish from the oven and pour the sauce over the fillets before serving.

Variations: Vary the flavor of this dish by adding herbs, artichokes or sliced kalamata olives.

Chicken Piccata

Serves: 4

4	(8-ounce) boneless, skinless, chicken or turkey breast
3	tablespoons flour
2	large eggs, lightly beaten
1 1/4	cups breadcrumbs or Panko (Italian seasoned, if available)
1/2	garlic salt
1/4	teaspoon black pepper
3	tablespoons unsalted butter, divided use
1	teaspoon extra virgin olive oil

Lemon Sauce

1	tablespoon freshly squeezed lemon juice
1	cup chicken broth or stock
1	tablespoon cornstarch mixed with one tablespoon cold water
1	tablespoon capers, drained and rinsed Cooked brown rice

Preheat the oven to 350°F. Lay chicken breasts flat on a cutting surface. Slice the breast horizontally into 2 filets. Place flour into a shallow dish. In a separate dish, whisk the eggs. In another dish, add the breadcrumbs, salt and pepper. Dredge the chicken in the flour, then the egg and then the breadcrumbs so it is coated on all sides. Heat 2 tablespoons butter and olive oil and sauté the breasts until golden on both sides, about 2 1/2 minutes on each side. Place chicken on an ovenproof dish and place in oven and bake 10 minutes until chicken is fully cooked.

Make sauce. Using the skillet with drippings, melt the remaining tablespoon butter and add lemon juice. Add chicken stock and half of the cornstarch mixture. Heat to boiling, whisking constantly. Add remaining cornstarch mixture if necessary. Before serving, add the capers. Serve over rice.

Spinach Stuffed Chicken Breasts with Parmesan
Serves: 6

6	(8-ounce) skinless, boneless chicken breasts
3/4	cup fresh spinach
	Lemon pepper

Parmesan Cream Sauce

2	tablespoons unsalted butter
2	teaspoons extra virgin olive oil
1/3	cup minced shallots (two medium shallots)
2	medium cloves garlic, minced
3	cups chicken broth or stock
¾	cup half & half
2/3	cup freshly grated Parmigiano-Reggiano cheese
2	tablespoons cornstarch mixed with 2 tablespoons cold water
	Cooked brown or wild rice blend

Preheat oven to 350°F. Pound the chicken breasts to an even thickness, using the flat side of a mallet. Divide spinach evenly and place on top of each breast and secure with a toothpick. Sprinkle with lemon pepper. Heat the butter and 1 teaspoon olive oil in a large skillet. Over medium heat, without burning the butter, brown breasts quickly on all sides. Remove chicken to an ovenproof 9 x 13-inch glass dish. Bake for 25 to 35 minutes until juices run clear when pierced with a fork. Make the sauce while the breasts are cooking. In the same pan, heat the remaining teaspoon of oil and add the shallots and garlic. Sauté until shallot is translucent. Add the chicken stock and bring to a boil. Add half & half, cheese and bring to boil. While whisking, add half of the cornstarch mixture. Add remainder if necessary. Sauce should thicken in approximately 2 minutes. Whisk sauce occasionally and reduce heat to low to hold warm. Slice chicken on the diagonal; serve over rice drizzled with the sauce.

Variation: Turkey cutlets may replace the chicken breasts. They are the leanest source of protein.

Goat Cheese Stuffed Chicken with Marsala Sauce
Serves: 6
Goat Cheese Stuffed Chicken

6	(8-ounce) skinless, boneless chicken breasts
1	(5-ounce) log goat cheese
1	tablespoon herbes de Provence
¼	cup diced dried plums (prunes)
2	tablespoons unsalted butter, divided use
1	teaspoon extra-virgin olive oil

Marsala Sauce

1/3	cup minced shallots (two medium shallots)
3	large cloves garlic, minced
2	cups Marsala wine
2	cups chicken broth or stock
1	teaspoon fresh rosemary
1	tablespoon cornstarch mixed with 1 tablespoon cold water
	Cooked brown or wild rice blend

Preheat the oven to 350°F. Pound the chicken breast to an even thickness using the flat side of a meat mallet. Mix goat cheese, herbes de Provence and prunes. Evenly distribute the goat cheese mixture and form six small logs of goat cheese. Place the logs in the middle of each breast and wrap the chicken around the log securing with a toothpick. In a large skillet, heat one tablespoon butter and olive oil. Over medium heat, brown the breasts quickly on all sides. Remove chicken rolls to an ovenproof dish. Bake in oven 25 to 35 minutes until juices run clear when pierced with a fork. Make the sauce. In the same pan, heat the remaining butter and add the shallots and garlic. Sauté until shallot is translucent. Add the Marsala and continue to cook until reduced by half (approximately 30 minutes). Add the broth and rosemary. Bring to boil. While whisking, add the cornstarch mixture Reduce heat and simmer, whisking to blend. Sauce should thicken in approximately 2 minutes. Whisk sauce occasionally and reduce heat to low to hold warm. Slice chicken on the diagonal; serve over rice drizzled with the sauce.

Indian Pepper Chicken

Serves: 6

12	skinless, bone-in chicken thighs, extra fat removed
1	tablespoons unsalted butter
2	teaspoons coarsely ground black peppercorns (see note)
2	cups plain nonfat yogurt
1	tablespoon cornstarch, divided use
1	tablespoon fresh minced ginger
1	tablespoon minced garlic
2	minced serrano chiles, seeds intact
2	teaspoons sea salt
3/4	teaspoon ground cumin
1	teaspoon ground coriander
1	cup fresh cilantro, chopped
	Cooked brown rice

Rinse the chicken and pat dry. Heat the butter in another small pan and toast the peppercorns for one minute, set aside. In a large saucepan, stir together yogurt, 2 teaspoons cornstarch and next six ingredients. Add the chicken and mix well. Marinate 30 minutes at room temperature. Cover and bring to boil over medium heat. Reduce the heat and simmer, turning the chicken occasionally. Chicken should simmer about 35 minutes. If there is a lot of liquid, leave the lid off while cooking. Reduce the heat, shaking pan occasionally until there is just one cup of liquid and chicken is no longer pin inside. If the sauce does not seem thick enough, mix the last teaspoon of cornstarch with teaspoon cold water and add it to the remaining liquid in pan and boil, stirring constantly. Scatter the cilantro over the top and lower heat. Pour the peppercorns over the chicken and gently mix in. Cover and let stand 5 minutes before serving. Serve the thighs over rice with the sauce.

Note: An inexpensive coffee grinder used for spices only is best for grinding the peppercorns to a coarse consistency.

Lettuce Wraps

Serves: 4

    1   tablespoon unsalted butter
    1   medium onion, chopped
    2   pounds ground turkey
    2   cloves garlic, chopped
    1   teaspoon ground cumin or more to taste
    1   (10.5 ounce) can Ro*Tel tomatoes (heat
         level desired)
    1   (15-ounce) can organic black beans, rinsed
         and drained
  1/2 cup frozen corn or peas
         Pepper, to taste
         Whole lettuce leaves

In a skillet, melt the butter and sauté the onion, adding meat and garlic once onion begins to turn translucent. Add the cumin, Ro*Tel, beans and vegetables. Put a lid on the skillet and cook until corn is tender and juice from Ro*tel has cooked down. Serve warm wrapped in a lettuce leaf. Thank you Vince for this healthy concoction!

*Variation: Whole wheat flour tortillas may replace lettuce. Fresh tomatoes (1/2 pound) can be used in place of Ro*Tel to reduce sodium, if desired.*

Sweet Potato-Black Bean Tostadas
Serves: 4

1	medium-sized sweet potato
1	(15-ounce) can organic black beans, rinsed and drained
1/3	cup water
1	pound ground turkey
1	(1.25-ounce) package low-sodium taco seasoning
1	1/2 cups part-skim cheddar cheese
8	tostada shells
2	cups leaf lettuce or fresh baby spinach, cut crosswise in 1/2-inch slices
2	medium tomatoes, seeded and diced in 1/4-inch pieces
	Hot sauce (optional)

Preheat oven to 350°F. Bake the sweet potato until tender when pierced with a fork about 75 minutes. Once slightly cooled, peel the potato and mash. Drain and rinse black beans. In a blender, combine potato, beans and 1/3 cup water until thickened and smooth. Keep warm until ready to serve. In a skillet, brown the meat and add seasoning and water as directed on the back of the package. Heat the tostada shells approximately 3 minutes. Spread the shell with beans and top with the meat, cheese, lettuce, tomato and sauce if desired.

Turkey and Black Bean Chili
Serves: 8

2	tablespoons unsalted butter
1	teaspoon extra-virgin olive oil
3	cups diced onion
2	pounds ground turkey
6	garlic cloves, minced
2	cups water
2	tablespoons ground cumin
2	tablespoons chili powder
2	teaspoons dried oregano
2	teaspoons sea salt
1	teaspoon cayenne pepper
3	(6-ounce) cans tomato paste
2	teaspoons turbinado or natural brown sugar
1	(28-ounce) can chopped tomatoes
3	cups diced red pepper
2	(15-ounce) cans organic black beans, rinsed and drained
2 3/4	cups beef broth
1	cup chopped fresh cilantro
	Cheddar cheese (optional)

Heat the butter and oil in a large pot over medium-high heat. Add onion and sauté about 3 minutes. Add the meat and garlic and continue to sauté until no pink remains in meat, stirring often so garlic does not brown. Add the 2 cups water; bring to boil. Add the spices. Reduce the heat, cover and simmer 10 minutes. Add the tomato paste, sugar and simmer 5 minutes. Add the tomatoes, peppers, beans and broth. Simmer a minimum of 30 minutes or until ready to serve. Serve topped with cilantro and cheddar cheese, if desired. This chili freezes well.

Asian Ginger Beef

Serves: 4

1	tablespoon sesame oil
1	(1-pound) sirloin steak, trimmed & sliced 1/8-inch thick
1/4	cup fresh minced ginger
2	large cloves garlic, minced
4	medium carrots, peeled and sliced
1	crown broccoli, tough stems removed, cut in florets
1	small yellow onion, julienne
1/3	cup less-sodium soy sauce
1/4	cup black bean sauce
1	serrano chile, seeds intact, minced (optional)
1/2	cup beef or vegetable broth
1/4	cup dry sherry
2	teaspoons cornstarch
1	red bell pepper, thinly sliced
	Cooked brown rice

In a large sauté pan, heat the sesame oil and add the meat. Brown the meat about 3 minutes on each side. Remove the meat to a platter. Add the ginger, garlic, and carrots. Stir-fry for 3 minutes. Add the broccoli and onions. Continue to stir-fry until the onions are translucent and broccoli is tender-crisp. Remove the broccoli with a slotted spoon and set aside. Mix soy sauce, black bean sauce, chile and beef broth. In a separate bowl, mix the sherry and cornstarch to a paste. Add the liquids and the cornstarch mixture to the pan. Bring to a boil. Add the red pepper; cook until just softened. Add the meat and broccoli back to the pan to reheat. Serve over rice.

Pasta with Seafood and Herbs

Serves: 2

8	ounces brown rice pasta
2	tablespoons unsalted butter
2	tablespoons extra virgin olive oil
2	tablespoons finely chopped shallots
2	garlic cloves, minced
3	baby bok choy or one regular sized (about 4 cups, sliced), tough ends removed
1/3	cup white wine
2	tablespoons heavy cream
2	tablespoons capers, drained and rinsed
1	tablespoon freshly squeezed lemon juice
1	pound seafood (orange roughy, tilapia or wild salmon), chopped into 1-inch pieces
1/4	cup chopped fresh basil
1/4	teaspoon fresh rosemary, chopped
1	tablespoon fresh oregano leaves, chopped
1/4	teaspoon dried thyme leaves
1/2	cup seeded chopped tomatoes
	Freshly grated Parmigiano-Reggiano (optional)

Boil the pasta according to package directions. Drain (do not rinse), set aside covered to keep warm. In a medium sauté pan, melt the butter and add olive oil. Add the shallots, garlic and bok choy and sauté about 3 minutes. Add the wine; reduce by half. Add the cream, capers, lemon, and fish. Continuing to stir; cook until fish is cooked through and no longer opaque. Add the herbs and tomatoes. Toss the mixture with the hot cooked pasta. Top with Parmigiano-Reggiano, if desired.

Pasta with Gorgonzola, Peppers and Tomatoes

Serves: 6

- 2 tablespoons unsalted butter
- 1 teaspoon extra-virgin olive oil
- 1 medium onion, diced
- 2 large cloves garlic, minced
- 1 red pepper, seeded and cut in chunk
  Pinch red pepper flakes
- 1 (28-ounce) can imported Italian plum tomatoes, cut in quarters
- 1 tablespoons balsamic vinegar
- 1 (4-ounce) package Gorgonzola cheese
- 2 tablespoons half-and-half
- 16 ounces cooked brown rice pasta
  Basil leaves, cut in thin strips (chiffonade), for garnish
  Freshly grated Parmigiano-Reggiano (optional)

Heat the butter and olive oil in a large skillet and sauté the onion, garlic, pepper and red pepper flakes until onions are translucent. Add the tomatoes with juice and balsamic; simmer on low. In a bowl, blend the cheese with half & half. Cook pasta according to package directions. Once pasta is cooked and drained (do not rinse), toss the cheese mixture with warm pasta. Serve with tomatoes over the top, sprinkled with fresh basil. Pass the Parmesan separately.

Pasta with Tomatoes and Goat Cheese

Serves: 4

2	tablespoons unsalted butter
1	teaspoon extra-virgin olive oil
2	garlic cloves, minced
2	medium shallots, minced
	Pinch red pepper flakes
1/2	cup grape tomatoes, halved
	Sea salt
	Black pepper
4	cups baby spinach
12	ounces (21/25 count) shrimp, defrosted
3	ounces goat cheese
12	ounces cooked brown rice pasta
1/3	cup grated Parmigiano-Reggiano
1	tablespoon fresh chopped mint

In a skillet, heat the butter and olive oil and sauté garlic cloves, shallots and red pepper flakes. Add the tomatoes and sprinkle with salt and pepper. Allow the tomatoes to lose some of their juices then add the spinach and cook until wilted. Add the shrimp and cook until pink and slightly coiled (about 3 minutes). Add the goat cheese and stir into blend. Combine the mixture with hot pasta and toss with Parmesan and mint.

Mustard-Glazed Grilled Asparagus

Serves: 6

1/4 cup mayonnaise (light may be used)
1/4 cup coarse-grained Dijon mustard
1/4 cup extra-virgin olive oil
2   tablespoons fresh squeezed lemon juice
1   garlic clove, minced or pressed
1   teaspoon sea salt
1   teaspoon ground black pepper
1   pound thick asparagus, trimmed

In a shallow glass dish, whisk the mayonnaise with the next six ingredients. Add the asparagus and toss to coat. Marinate asparagus for 30 minutes. Grill the asparagus over moderately high heat, turning occasionally until spears are tender, approximately 6 minutes.

Portobello Mushrooms with Sweet Potatoes

Serves: 8

1	large sweet potato, peeled and diced into 1-inch pieces
4	medium russet potatoes, peeled and diced into1-inch pieces
6	whole peeled garlic cloves
1	bay leaf
1	teaspoon sea salt
3	tablespoons unsalted butter, divided use
2	large eggs, beaten
1/4	cup freshly grated Parmigiano-Reggiano Sea salt and pepper, to taste
8	medium portobello mushrooms, cleaned
2	tablespoons extra virgin olive oil, divided use
3	cups fresh baby spinach
1/2	cup finely chopped yellow onion

Preheat the oven to 400°F. In a large pot or Dutch oven, add potatoes, garlic and bay leaf. Fill pan 2/3 full of cold water, enough to cover potatoes. Add salt and bring to a boil. Boil the potatoes for 15 to 20 minutes or until tender. Remove the bay leaf. Drain potatoes, add 2 tablespoons butter and with a potato masher, mash the potatoes and garlic until smooth. Cool slightly; beat in eggs and cheese. Add salt and pepper, to taste. Remove the mushrooms stems. With a spoon, remove the gills gently. Set the caps aside. Chop the stems. Heat remaining table-spoon butter in a large skillet and add the spinach, onion and stems; sauté the mixture 5 minutes and remove from heat. Drizzle remaining tablespoon olive oil over the rounded sides of mushroom caps and distribute evenly using a pastry brush. Place mushrooms on a baking sheet gill sides up and bake 10 minutes. Remove from the oven and reduce temperature to 350°F. Distribute the spinach mixture evenly over the gill side of caps. Use a star piping tip and fill a disposable piping bag with the potato mixture. Pipe the potato mixture on top of the spinach. Bake 25 minutes. A beautiful side for any grilled or roasted meat!

Tools: Star pastry tip and piping bag

Potato and Yam Gratin
Serves: 6

2   medium-sized red skinned potatoes,
     unpaired
1   yam or sweet potato
     Dash nutmeg
3/4 cup heavy cream
1/2 teaspoon white pepper
1/2 teaspoon sea salt
1/4 cup chopped fresh chives
1/2 cup freshly grated Parmesan cheese
     Butter

Preheat the oven to 350°F and butter a 9 x 13-inch pan. Combine the salt, pepper, nutmeg and cream. Cut the potatoes in 1/4-inch slices. Peel the sweet potato and cut in 1/4-inch slices. Cover the bottom of the pan with the potatoes alternating the sweet and regular. Drizzle the cream mixture over and sprinkle with Parmesan and chives. Cover with foil the dull side out for 30 minutes. Remove foil and bake for another 30 or until potatoes are tender.

Naturally Sweet Carrots

Serves: 8

2   pounds carrots, peeled and sliced into uniform pieces
1   tablespoon unsalted butter

Place the carrots and butter in a saucepan over very low heat and cover with a tight-fitting lid. The carrots will slowly steam in their own moisture and turn a beautiful orange and be sweet. Shake the pan from time to time. After 10 minutes on a low heat, check to see if the temperature is correct. Lift the lid and you should see steam and barely hear the carrots cooking. If there is no steam, raise the heat, but if you hear sizzling, reduce the heat. Cook until the carrots are tender. This process can take from 25 to 40 minutes. When the carrots are finished cooking they should be tender and only a small amount of butter that is clear should remain in the bottom of the pan. Toss the carrots with the butter in the pan and serve hot.

Portabellos with Spinach
Serves: 4
Portabellos
- 1 large portabello mushroom
- 2 tablespoons honey
- 1 tablespoon less-sodium soy sauce
- ¼ cup olive oil, divided use
- 1/8 teaspoon ground ginger

Spinach
- 1 (9-ounce) bag spinach
- 2 tablespoons water
- 2 tablespoons pine nuts
- 1/3 cup dried cranberries (Craisins)

Preheat oven to 350°F. With a spoon, gently remove the gills. Discard gills. Toast the pine nuts in the oven (or stovetop) approximately 3 to 4 minutes until lightly golden. Mix the honey, soy sauce, olive oil (reserve one tablespoon) and ginger together. Marinate the mushrooms in the mixture one hour at room temperature. Slice the mushroom and sauté in reserved olive oil. In a separate pan, bring the tablespoon of water to boil and add the spinach, covering with lid. Steam the spinach on low heat, 5 minutes. Toss the spinach with the mushroom, pine nuts and the cranberries. A good accompaniment to grilled meats!

Oven-Roasted Vegetables
Serves: 8

Assorted vegetables (small whole potatoes or peeled, quartered sweet potatoes; peeled, quartered onions or shallots; red peppers, seeded and cut in chunks, sliced fennel, carrots, parsnips and asparagus or broccoli crowns)

2 tablespoons extra virgin olive oil
1 teaspoon sea salt
1/4 teaspoon black pepper
1/4 teaspoon dried marjoram
1 tablespoon minced or pressed garlic

Preheat oven to 450°F. Wash and clean the vegetables. Toss all the vegetables with olive oil and sprinkle with salt, pepper, marjoram and garlic. Set tender vegetables such as asparagus and red peppers aside. In a shallow baking dish or on a jelly roll pan, arrange vegetables in a single layer. Roast 20 minutes and stir. Add asparagus and peppers continue to roast an additional 10 minutes.

Note: Sturdy fresh herbs like rosemary and thyme may be included in this recipe. Potatoes should be almost finished roasting, tender when pierced with a fork, before adding the vegetables that roast more quickly, such as asparagus. Kale (leaves sliced) and cauliflower (broken in florets) are two of my favorites vegetables roasted by themselves.

Desserts
Steel Cut Oat and Cranberry Cookies
Makes: 24 Cookies

1	cup pure applesauce
2	large eggs
1	teaspoon vanilla
1/2	cup turbinado or raw sugar
1 1/2	cups whole-wheat flour
2	cups steel-cut oats
1/2	teaspoon sea salt
1	teaspoon baking powder
1/4	teaspoon baking soda
2	teaspoons cinnamon
1	cup walnut halves, toasted (optional) and coarsely chopped
1	cup dried cranberries (Craisins)
	Coconut oil for greasing cookie sheet

Preheat the oven to 375°F. Mix the applesauce, eggs, vanilla and sugar together in a large bowl. Add the dry ingredients, nuts and dried cranberries. Use a small amount of the coconut oil to grease the cookie sheet. Drop cookies by tablespoons onto sheet. Bake approximately 15 to 20 minutes. Cool and store in airtight container. These freeze well.

Chocolate Pots de Crème

2 1/2	cups chilled heavy cream, divided use
1	tablespoon plus 1 teaspoon instant espresso powder
5	ounces bittersweet chocolate chips or bars, finely chopped
6	egg yolks from large eggs, room temperature
2	tablespoons sugar
1	teaspoon vanilla extract
	Pinch sea salt
	Stevia, to taste for whipping cream
6	chocolate covered coffee beans (optional)

Place baking rack in center of oven and pre-heat the oven to 325°F. Combine 2 cups of cream and espresso powder in a heavy medium saucepan. Bring the mixture to a simmer (180°F) while dissolving the espresso. Stir the chocolate into the cream until melted and smooth; set aside. In a large bowl, whisk the egg yolks, sugar, vanilla and salt until well blended. Whisk in the chocolate mixture. Strain the liquid into a 4 cup measuring cup. Place six ¾ cup ramekins in a glass 9 x 13-inch baking dish. Divide the mixture evenly into cups. Place dish on middle rack and with a pitcher, pour enough hot water to come halfway up the outside of the ramekins. Cover the top of pan with aluminum foil. Bake until the custard is just set around the edges, approximately 25 minutes. Carefully remove the pan from the oven. Remove the dishes from the pan and allow them to cool. Cover and chill in the refrigerator 2 hours or overnight. Whip the remaining 1/2 cup cream and sweeten with Stevia. Place cream in pastry bag with star tip. Pipe one star on top of each dish and top with chocolate covered coffee bean if desired.

Note: *Stevia* is a genus of about 240 species of herbs and shrubs in the sunflower family Use sparingly due to the concentration.

Tools: (optional) Star pastry tip and piping bag Six ¾ cup ovenproof glass ramekins

Visit www.recipeforlife.biz for more recipes!

"Live with intention.
Walk to the edge.
Listen hard.
Practice wellness.
Play with abandon.
Laugh.
Choose with no regret.
Continue to learn.
Appreciate your friends.
Do what you love.
Live as if this is all there is. "

Mary Anne Radmacher